No Backbone!
The World of Invertebrates

Killer Bees

by Meish Goldish

Consultant: Brian V. Brown
Curator, Entomology Section
Natural History Museum of Los Angeles County

BEARPORT
PUBLISHING

NEW YORK, NEW YORK

Credits

Cover, © age fotostock/SuperStock; 4–5, © REUTERS/Eliana Aponte; 6–7, © AGStockUSA/Darwin Dale; 8T, © Pascal Goetgheluck/ARDEA.com; 8B, © CAROLINA BIOL./OSF/Animals Animals Earth Scenes; 9, © Kenneth Lorenzen; 10, © Juniors Bildarchiv/Oxford Scientific/Photolibrary; 11, © age fotostock/SuperStock; 12T, © John B Free/Nature Picture Library; 12M, © Anne & Jacques Six/Auscape; 12B, © Anne & Jacques Six/Auscape; 13, © Steve Hopkin/Ardea; 14, © James Robinson/Animals Animals Earth Scenes; 15, © Stephen Dalton/Photo Researchers, Inc.; 16, © REUTERS/Eliana Aponte; 17, © Kevin Schafer/CORBIS; 19, © Lorraine Beaman, USDA Honey Bee Lab, Bugwood.org; 21, © AP Images/Texas Cooperative Extension, Jerrold Summerlin; 22TL, © Michael Durham/Minden Pictures; 22TR, © James H. Robinson/Oxford Scientific/Photolibrary; 22BL, © Frank Greenaway/Dorling Kindersley/Getty Images; 22BR, © Michael Durham/Minden Pictures; 23TL, © Jim Wehtje/Photodisc Green/Getty Images; 23TR, © Juniors Bildarchiv/Oxford Scientific/Photolibrary; 23BL, © AGStockUSA/Darwin Dale; 23BR, © Pascal Goetgheluck/ARDEA.com.

Publisher: Kenn Goin
Editorial Director: Adam Siegel
Creative Director: Spencer Brinker
Design: Dawn Beard Creative
Photo Researcher: Nancy Tobin

Library of Congress Cataloging-in-Publication Data

Goldish, Meish.
Killer bees / by Meish Goldish.
    p. cm. — (No backbone! The world of invertebrates)
Includes bibliographical references and index.
ISBN-13: 978-1-59716-581-5 (library binding)
ISBN-10: 1-59716-581-6 (library binding)
1. Africanized honeybee—Juvenile literature. I. Title.

QL568.A6G63 2008
595.79'9—dc22

2007034599

For more information, write to Bearport Publishing Company, Inc., 101 Fifth Avenue, Suite 6R, New York, New York 10003. Printed in the United States of America.

10 9 8 7 6 5 4 3 2 1

Contents

Little Killers

Bees are **insects** that can fly and sting.

Usually only one bee at a time attacks a person or animal.

There is a kind of bee, however, that is different.

Thousands of these insects attack together.

They are called killer bees because their attacks can be deadly.

In the past 50 years, about 1,000 people have died from killer bee attacks.

A Bee's Body

Killer bees are a kind of honey bee.

Like all bees, they have six legs and four wings.

On their heads are two antennas that they use for smelling.

Female killer bees also have a sharp **stinger** to use in an attack.

Bees and all other insects have a hard covering called an exoskeleton. The exoskeleton protects the insect's body and keeps it from drying out.

antennas

wings

legs

7

Getting Stung

A bee's stinger has tiny, sharp hooks in it.

The bee pushes its stinger into the skin of an enemy.

Poison flows from the stinger into the victim's body.

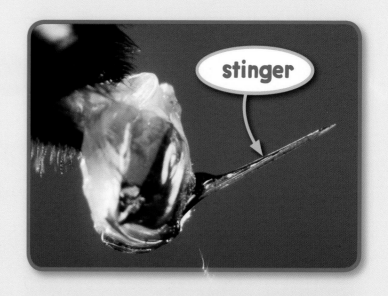

stinger

stinger

When a bee stings someone, its stinger breaks off from its body. The bee then bleeds to death.

stinger

In the Hive

Killer bees live together in a **hive**.

Each bee has its own job to do.

One female, called the queen, lays all the eggs.

Other female bees, called workers, build the hive and feed the babies.

Males called drones leave the hive to mate with other queens.

killer bee hive

A killer bee hive can have thousands of workers.

queen bee

worker bees

11

Changing Forms

In the hive, a baby killer bee starts out as an egg.

After three days, the egg hatches.

A tiny worm-like creature called a larva comes out.

After a week, the larva changes into a mummy-like form called a pupa.

Over the next ten days, the pupa changes into an adult bee.

A queen killer bee can lay up to 6,000 eggs a day. That is twice as many eggs as other honey bees lay.

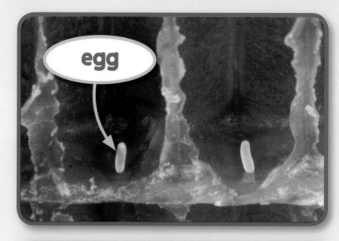

egg

larva

pupa

adult honey bee

Honey Makers

Like all honey bees, a killer bee makes honey.

First it sips a sweet liquid called nectar from flowers.

Juices inside the bee's body mix with the nectar.

The bee spits up this mixture and stores it in the hive.

Over time it thickens and turns into honey.

Honey bees are the only insect that make food that people eat.

Going Wild

Like other honey bees, killer bees defend their hives.

They chase and try to sting any person or animal that comes too close.

A killer bee's sting isn't more deadly than a regular honey bee's sting.

The killers cause more harm because they sting as a group.

One attacking group can be made up of thousands of killer bees.

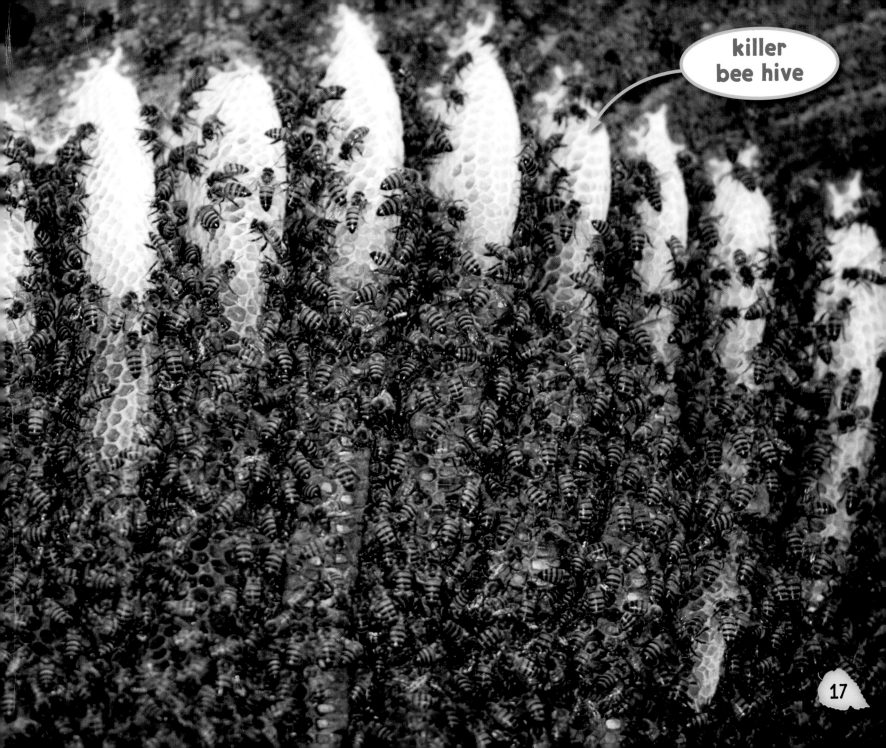

A New Kind of Bee

Before 1956, there was no such thing as killer bees.

That year, scientists mated honey bees in Brazil with bees from Africa to create a new kind of bee.

They hoped that these bees would make more honey.

The next year, some of the new bees escaped and spread across South America.

By the 1990s, the killer bees had flown north to Mexico and into the United States.

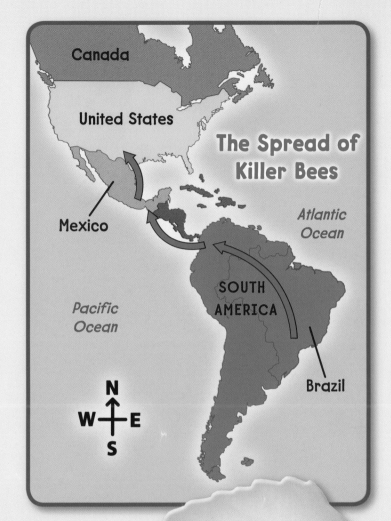

The Spread of Killer Bees

Most of the deadly killer bee attacks so far have taken place in Brazil and other countries south of the United States.

Killer Bees Today

Killer bees are not as dangerous as people once feared.

The bees have not spread across most of the United States.

The main reason is that the weather is too cold for them.

Yet people should still learn as much as they can about killer bees.

Then they will have a better chance of staying safe—and far away—from these little killers!

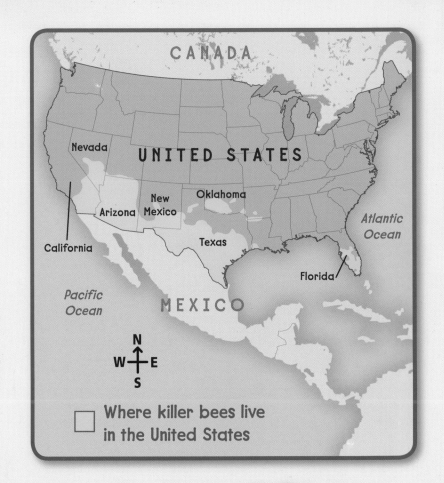

Today, killer bees can be found in several states, including Texas, New Mexico, Arizona, Nevada, California, Oklahoma, and Florida.

An animal that has a skeleton with a **backbone** inside its body is a *vertebrate* (VUR-tuh-brit). Mammals, birds, fish, reptiles, and amphibians are all vertebrates.

An animal that does not have a skeleton with a backbone inside its body is an *invertebrate* (in-VUR-tuh-brit). More than 95 percent of all kinds of animals on Earth are invertebrates.

Some invertebrates, such as insects and spiders, have hard skeletons—called exoskeletons—outside their bodies. Other invertebrates, such as worms and jellyfish, have soft, squishy bodies with no exoskeletons to protect them.

Here are four insects that are closely related to killer bees. Like all insects, they are invertebrates.

Bumble Bee

Carpenter Bee

Hornet

Yellow Jacket

Glossary

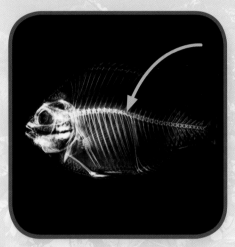

backbone
(BAK-*bohn*)
a group of
connected bones
that run along
the backs of some
animals, such as
dogs, cats, and fish;
also called a spine

hive (HIVE)
a nest that bees
build and use to
raise young and
store honey

insects (IN-sekts)
small animals that
have six legs, three
main body parts,
two antennas, and a
hard covering called
an exoskeleton

stinger
(STING-ur)
the sharp,
pointed part of
a killer bee used
in an attack

Index

Read More

Landau, Elaine. *Killer Bees*. Berkeley Heights, NJ: Enslow Publishers (2003).

Markle, Sandra. *Outside and Inside Killer Bees.* New York: Walker Books (2004).

Learn More Online

To learn more about killer bees, visit

www.bearportpublishing.com/NoBackbone-Insects

About the Author

Meish Goldish has written more than 100 books for children. He lives in Brooklyn, New York.